Olivia and the Pacifier Fairy

No More Binkie

By Andrea Locket

OLIVIA LOVED HER PACIFIER SHE HAD IT WITH HER ALL THE TIME.

SHE EVEN HAD IT WHEN SHE GOT HER TOY BOX OUT TO PLAY WITH HER BEAR AND STACKING BRICKS.

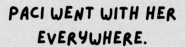

PACI WENT WITH HER
EVERYWHERE.

SHE'D NOT EVEN TAKE IT OUT
WHEN SHE HAD A BATH!

IT WAS MAKING MOM A LITTLE SAD.
SHE KNEW OLIVA HAD A
WONDERFUL SMILE, BUT NOBODY
EVER GOT TO SEE IT. HER LOVELY
SMILE WAS HIDDEN BEHIND HER
PACIFIER.

MOM TRIED TO PERSUADE OLIVIA TO GIVE UP HER PACI. BUT IT DIDN'T WORK. OLIVIA HAD PACIFIERS HIDDEN ALL OVER THE HOUSE.

DID YOU FIND THEM ALL?

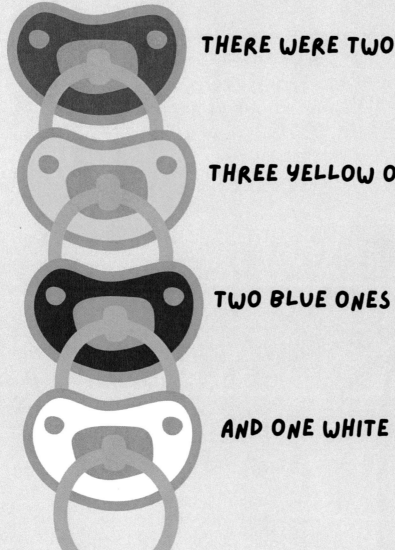

THERE WERE TWO RED ONES

THREE YELLOW ONES

TWO BLUE ONES

AND ONE WHITE ONE

MOM'S LETTER ARRIVES IN
FAIRYLAND

MOM'S LETTER MAKES IT ALL THE
WAY TO FAIRYLAND.

EMILY THE UNICORN DELIVERS IT
TO SOPHIE THE PACIFIER FAIRY.

SOPHIE IS THE BEST PACIFIER
FAIRY THERE HAS EVER BEEN

SOPHIE READS MOM'S LETTER

SOPHIE LAUGHS WHEN SHE READS
THE LETTER. SHE CAN REMEMBER
OLIVIA'S MOM. ONE OF THE
TOUGHEST CASES SHE'D EVER HAD.
OLIVIA'S MOM HADN'T WANTED TO
GIVE UP HER PACIFIER WHEN SHE
WAS LITTLE.
SOPHIE SETS OFF TO VISIT OLIVIA.

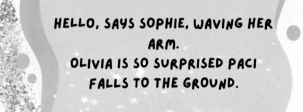

HELLO, SAYS SOPHIE, WAVING HER ARM.
OLIVIA IS SO SURPRISED PACI FALLS TO THE GROUND.

ALL AROUND OLIVIA THERE ARE GLITTERING STARS AND PUFFS OF MAGIC DUST.

"YOUR MOM WROTE ME A LETTER AND ASKED ME TO CALL. SHE WANTED ME TO RELEASE YOUR SMILE,' SAYS SOPHIE.

"I DON'T UNDERSTAND,' SAYS OLIVIA. "I'VE NOT LOST MY SMILE AND IT'S NOT TRAPPED ANYWHERE?"

SOPHIE LAUGHS, AND WHISPERS, "YOU NEED TO STOP HIDING YOUR BRIGHT SMILE BEHIND A PACI."

"IT'S TRAPPED BEHIND PACI AND WE CAN'T SEE WHETHER YOU ARE HAPPY OR SAD," SOPHIE EXPLAINED. "AND THE DREAM FAIRY WON'T KNOW WHAT SORT OF DREAMS TO BRING YOU IF SHE CAN'T SEE YOUR SMILE."

"I DIDN'T KNOW THAT," SAID OLIVIA. "BUT I DON'T WANT TO GIVE PACI UP, I LIKE IT. I ALWAYS HAVE IT."

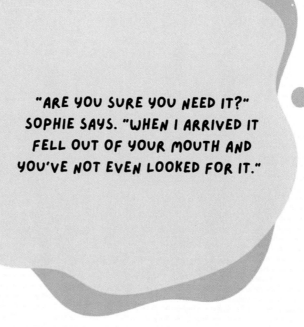

"ARE YOU SURE YOU NEED IT?" SOPHIE SAYS. "WHEN I ARRIVED IT FELL OUT OF YOUR MOUTH AND YOU'VE NOT EVEN LOOKED FOR IT."

"WOW! YOU ARE RIGHT. I HADN'T NOTICED IT WAS MISSING AT ALL," SAID OLIVIA.

"IF YOU FIND ALL YOUR PACI'S AND PUT THEM IN A BOX OUTSIDE YOUR ROOM I'LL LEAVE YOU THIS MAGICAL FAIRY GIFT IN THE MORNING," SOPHIE SAYS.

CAN YOU CHECK? HAS OLIVIA PUT
THEM ALL IN THE BOX?
THERE SHOULD BE
THREE YELLOW ONES
TWO RED ONES
TWO BLUE ONES
AND ONE WHITE ONE

SOPHIE CHECKS THEY ARE ALL
THERE. THEN PICKS UP THE BOX
AND FLYS UP INTO THE AIR. SHE'S
LEFT A MAGICAL GIFT FOR OLIVIA.

INSIDE IS A MAGICAL TEDDY FOR OLIVIA. SHE CAN HUG TEDDY ALL NIGHT AND HE'LL MAKE SURE SHE NEVER THINKS ABOUT HER PACI AGAIN.

WHY DON'T YOU GATHER UP ALL YOUR PACIFIERS AND POP THEM IN A BOX OUTSIDE YOUR BEDROOM DOOR? SOPHIE THE PACIFIER FAIRY MIGHT LEAVE YOU A LITTLE GIFT AS WELL.

🎁

Made in the USA
Las Vegas, NV
21 April 2024

88958513R00017